# What Catholics Believe

## A Pocket Catechism

Mike Aquilina

Fr. Kris D. Stubna

Our Sunday Visitor Publishing Division
Our Sunday Visitor, Inc.
Huntington, Indiana 46750

*Nihil Obstat:*
Rev. James Wehner, S.T.L.
*Imprimatur:*
✠Most Reverend William J. Winter, V.G., S.T.D.
Auxiliary Bishop and Vicar General
Diocese of Pittsburgh
June 30, 1998

The *nihil obstat* and *imprimatur* are official declarations that a book or pamphlet is free from doctrinal or moral error. It is not implied that those who have granted the *nihil obstat* and *imprimatur* agree with the contents, opinions, or statements expressed. Scripture text used in this work may be verbatim or paraphrased and are taken from the *New American Bible with Revised New Testament*, copyright © 1986, 1970, and from the *Revised Standard Version, Catholic Edition*, copyright © 1965 and 1966 by the Division of Christian Education of the National Council of the Churches of Christ.

The text of this work is based on the teaching of the *Catechism of the Catholic Church* for use in the United States of America, copyright © 1994, United States Catholic Conference — Libreria Editrice Vaticana. Used with permission. If any copyrighted materials have been inadvertently used in this work without proper credit being given in one manner or another, please notify Our Sunday Visitor in writing so that future printings of this book may be corrected accordingly.

ISBN: 087973-574-0
LCCCN: 98-67817

Cover Design by Tyler Ottinger

Printed in the United States of America

DEDICATED TO OUR PARENTS,
WHO TAUGHT US
THE CATHOLIC FAITH,
SOMETIMES USING WORDS

# TABLE OF CONTENTS

PREFACE / 5
INTRODUCTION / 7
PART ONE: THE CREED / 9
PART TWO: THE SACRAMENTS / 19
PART THREE: THE MORAL LIFE / 41
PART FOUR: PRAYER / 59

A TREASURY OF PRAYERS / 63

A CLOSER LOOK AT THE MASS / 74

WHAT IS THE SACRAMENT OF
RECONCILIATION? / 91

HOW TO MAKE A GOOD
CONFESSION / 97

THE RITE OF RECONCILIATION / 100

HOW TO MAKE AN EXAMINATION
OF CONSCIENCE / 103

THOUGHTS ON CHRISTIAN
FRIENDSHIP / 109

# PREFACE

One of the challenges that the *Catechism of the Catholic Church*, promulgated by our Holy Father, Pope John Paul II, as a normative summary of our Catholic Faith, presents is the need to disseminate at every level of catechesis and in a variety of ways the one same content of our Faith. Father Kris Stubna and Mike Aquilina have taken on this task with precision in *What Catholics Believe*.

Here we find in summary fashion the essential elements of the Faith presented in a way that permits someone being initiated into the Faith to grasp quickly and concisely what the Church teaches. What is particularly attractive about *What Catholics Believe* is the format of question and answer to the questions that continually arise as people attempt to grow more deeply in their understanding of the Faith. Enriching the work is "A Treasury of Prayers" with its storehouse of beloved and well-used Catholic prayers.

Anyone who has attempted to explain the Mass to someone attending for the first time will recognize the value of the section "A Closer Look at the Mass," which is a rich source of information for both neophytes and daily communicants.

As we move into the next millennium with its emphasis on evangelization — an outreach to many who have drifted away from the Faith — the questions that arise will find initial answers in this handy, trustworthy catechetical tool. As the Introduction to this work reminds us, one should turn to the *Catechism of the Catholic Church* for a complete treatment of any of the topics touched on here.

In recommending *What Catholics Believe*, I also ask God's blessings on those who use it in the catechetical effort to help achieve that new evangelization that is so much a part of the need of our time and the work of building up Christ's kingdom.

✠Donald W. Wuerl
Bishop of Pittsburgh

# INTRODUCTION

This book is neither a beginning nor an end.

Perhaps you are taking your first steps in exploring the Catholic Faith. Maybe you are trying to continue study you set aside long ago. Or perhaps you are looking for answers to urgent questions in your life. In any case, your impulse to seek is itself a grace from God, who will guide you as long as you sincerely and prayerfully seek to know Him, love Him, and do His will.

St. Augustine said, long ago, that our deepest desire is to "look upon one who looks back in love." Such love, endless and perfect, we will find only in God, and our hearts are restless until they rest in Him.

The Catholic Church is the ordinary way Jesus established for people to find peace in God. The Church is a mother and a teacher; the Church is a family and a home. The Church is a people on pilgrimage toward heaven.

We all find our way to God in the company of other believers and seekers. We hope this catechism will press you on: to find companionship in the Church, in your local parish; to worship with others; to attend the liturgy and pray the Mass deeply; to meditate on what you read here; to pursue further study within the Church; to ask questions of Catholic priests and teachers; to make your confession; to begin spiritual direction; to love others and love the Lord your God.

In short, we hope this little book will help you to take the next step you need to take, whatever that may be. For there is no standing still in the spiritual life. We either move forward or we fall behind.

You need not walk alone. We are with you for this little bit of the way. God is with you all the way, and so is His Church.

Seek Him.

— *The Authors*

# PART
# ONE

# THE
# CREED

*1. Who are you?*
My name is _____. I am a
child of God, created in His image and
likeness.

*2. Who is God?*
God is Love. Out of love, He made the
world and everything in it. Out of love
He made me and watches over me con-
stantly.

*3. Why did God make you?*
God made me to know Him, to love
Him, and to serve Him here on earth,

so that I may live with Him forever in heaven.

*4. What is the Holy Trinity?*
The Holy Trinity is the mystery of God. God is a Trinity because He is three Persons — Father, Son, and Holy Spirit — yet one God.

*5. Who is God the Father?*
God the Father is the first person of the Holy Trinity. He is a true and perfect Father, who guards us, His children, guides us, is always attentive to us, and provides for our needs.

*6. Who is Jesus?*
Jesus is the eternal Son of God, the second person of the Holy Trinity, who came into the world to save us from sin and show us the way to heaven. Jesus is true God and true man.

*7. How was Jesus born into this world?*
By the power of the Holy Spirit, Jesus became man and was born to the Virgin Mary. When God became man, He became our brother.

*8. How did Jesus live?*
Jesus worked, studied, and prayed as we all must do. He lived with His parents, Mary and Joseph, as an obedient and loving son.

*9. What are miracles?*
Miracles are acts of God. They show that God's power is greater than every other power, even the power of nature.

*10. Did Jesus perform miracles?*
Jesus performed many miracles. He changed water into wine, He healed the sick, He brought dead people to life,

and He fed thousands of people with a few loaves of bread.

*11. How did Jesus die?*
Jesus died on the Cross. People who did not believe in Jesus put Him to death. But Jesus still loved them. He said, "Forgive them, Father, for they do not know what they are doing."

*12. Why did Jesus die on the Cross?*
Jesus died on the Cross for my sake. He died to make up for all my sins and to open the gates of heaven for all of God's people.

*13. What happened after Jesus died?*
His mother and His friends laid Him in a tomb. After three days, Jesus rose from the dead. We call this the Resurrection. We celebrate the Resurrection on Easter Sunday.

*14. What is the Ascension?*

Forty days after rising from the dead, Jesus ascended to heaven, where He sits at the right hand of God the Father forever.

*15. Who were the apostles?*

The apostles were twelve men Jesus called to be His special friends and leaders in His Church. He sent them to every corner of the world to tell His good news.

*16. Who was St. Peter?*

St. Peter was the man Jesus chose to lead His Church. St. Peter was the first pope.

*17. What is a pope?*

Following after St. Peter, the pope is the supreme head of the Church on earth.

*18. Who are the bishops?*

The bishops are successors to the apostles. They teach, guide, and sanctify the people of God throughout the world.

*19. Who is the Holy Spirit?*

The Holy Spirit is the third person of the Holy Trinity. Jesus sent the Holy Spirit to His apostles on Pentecost, ten days after Jesus' Ascension. He continues to fill believers with His Spirit today.

*20. What does the Holy Spirit do?*

The Holy Spirit gives us the power to be faithful to God and to do all God asks of us. The Holy Spirit comes to us at baptism and at confirmation.

*21. What is the Church?*

The Church is the Living Body of Jesus

today. It is made up of all God's people. Jesus made the Church to be the ordinary way people could come to know God and be saved.

## 22. Why do we go to Church?

We go to Church to receive God's grace, especially in His Body and Blood in Holy Communion. We go to Church to gather with the people of God, to thank God for His gifts, and to take part in — to remember and give thanks for — the great sacrifice of Jesus on the Cross, which is made present in the Mass.

## 23. Who is the Blessed Virgin Mary?

The Blessed Virgin Mary is the Mother of Jesus. Because Jesus is God the Son, we call her the Mother of God. She is Mother of the Church and our mother, too.

*24. Why is Mary important?*
Mary is the model disciple, who gave God perfect obedience, always saying yes to Him. She was chosen, from all time, to bear God into the world.

*25. What is the Rosary?*
The Rosary is a series of prayers, counted on beads, which we offer to Mary as we think about the life of Jesus.

*26. What is a saint?*
The saints are Christians who have died and joined God in heaven. We honor them because they lived holy lives.

*27. Why do we pray to saints?*
Our Faith tells us that in heaven the saints pray for us on earth. Just as we might ask our best friend on earth to pray for us, we ask these good friends in heaven to pray for us.

*28. What happens when someone dies?*
People who follow God's will go to God at the end of their days on earth. His mercy purifies them of their sins, so that they can live in His presence.

*29. What is heaven?*
Heaven is life with God in His Kingdom forever. It is a state of total joy and peace, where there is no suffering.

*30. What is purgatory?*
Purgatory is the purification a soul goes through after death so that it can enter heaven.

*31. What is hell?*
Hell is a state of eternal punishment for people who die in serious sin, choosing not to love God or follow His commandments.

*32. What are angels?*

Angels are pure spirits without bodies. They serve as God's special messengers and helpers. The Bible mentions three archangels by name: Gabriel, Raphael, and Michael.

*33. What is a guardian angel?*

Guardian angels watch over us, helping us to do good and avoid evil. God gives everyone a guardian angel.

# PART TWO

# THE SACRAMENTS

*34. What is a sacrament?*
A sacrament is an outward sign instituted by Jesus to give grace. Through the sacraments, Jesus touches and blesses our lives.

*35. What is grace?*
Grace is our sharing in the life of God.

*36. How do we receive God's grace?*
God gives us grace as a free gift. Grace comes to us in many ways through the Holy Spirit, but most especially we receive this grace in the Church and her sacraments.

*37. How many sacraments are there?*
There are seven sacraments. They are baptism, confirmation, Holy Eucharist, penance, marriage, holy orders, and anointing of the sick.

*38. Where do the sacraments get their power to give grace?*
The power comes from Jesus' own life, especially His suffering, death, and resurrection. God's power works through the sacraments in spite of our own weakness.

*39. Do we always receive grace in the sacraments?*
The sacraments always give grace. But we have to be ready to receive that grace. We need to prepare our hearts so that we are in a state of grace.

*40. What is the state of grace?*
Living as God wishes us to live, free from mortal sin.

*41. Are the sacraments necessary for salvation?*
Yes. Jesus made the sacraments as the ordinary way to salvation. In His mercy, God gives his graces in extraordinary ways, but the sacraments remain the normal way people are saved.

*42. Where are the sacraments found?*
The sacraments are celebrated within the Church Jesus founded, the Catholic Church.

*43. Who ordinarily administers the sacraments?*
The ordinary minister of the sacraments is a bishop or a priest, who acts in the person of Jesus Christ.

*44. How often can we receive the sacraments?*

Some sacraments can be received only once because they leave a permanent spiritual mark on the Christian's soul. They are baptism, confirmation, and holy orders. Other sacraments should be received frequently, especially penance and Holy Eucharist.

*45. How are the sacraments divided?*

They are the sacraments of initiation (baptism, confirmation, and Holy Eucharist), the sacraments of healing (penance and anointing of the sick), and the sacraments at the service of communion (marriage and holy orders).

*46. What is baptism?*

Baptism is the sacrament that takes away original sin and makes us sons and daughters of God. By baptism we become members of the Church.

### 47. What is original sin?

It is the sin of the first humans, our first parents, who disobeyed God. All people share in the effects and the guilt of that sin: suffering, illness, death, and the tendency to sin. The guilt of original sin can only be removed by baptism.

### 48. How is baptism celebrated?

Water is poured over the head of the person, while the minister of baptism says, "I baptize you in the name of the Father, and of the Son, and of the Holy Spirit." The person is then anointed with holy chrism. The baptized person receives a white garment and a candle, meaning that he or she is now a child of God, enlightened by Jesus.

*49. Who can receive baptism?*

Anyone, at any age, can be baptized. Adults enter the Church through the Rite of Christian Initiation for Adults. Infants should receive baptism as soon as possible after their birth.

*50. Why does the Church baptize babies?*

Jesus said, "Let the little children come to Me, and do not hinder them." Every person is in need of God's grace. Every baby born should be set free from original sin and enabled to live as God wants us to live.

*51. What is confirmation?*

Confirmation is the sacrament through which we receive the gifts and the fruits of the Holy Spirit, strengthening us to be witnesses of Jesus Christ.

*52. What are the gifts of the Holy Spirit?*
There are seven gifts of the Holy Spirit: wisdom, understanding, counsel, fortitude, knowledge, piety, and fear of the Lord.

*53. What are the fruits of the Holy Spirit?*
The fruits of the Holy Spirit are charity, joy, peace, patience, kindness, goodness, generosity, gentleness, faithfulness, modesty, self-control, and chastity.

*54. Who can receive confirmation?*
Every baptized person should receive the sacrament of confirmation.

*55. What does confirmation do?*
By the power of the Holy Spirit, confirmation unites us more closely with

Jesus and the Church, giving us courage to share and to defend the Faith.

*56. Who administers confirmation?*
Usually, the bishop administers confirmation.

*57. How does the bishop give confirmation?*
The bishop extends his hands over each person to be confirmed, anoints the forehead with holy chrism, and prays, "Be sealed with the gift of the Holy Spirit."

*58. What is the Holy Eucharist?*
The Holy Eucharist is the sacrament which contains the Body, Blood, Soul, and Divinity of Jesus Christ under the form (or "species") of bread and wine.

*59. When did Jesus give us the Eucharist?*

Jesus gave us the Eucharist on Holy Thursday, at the Last Supper.

*60. How did Jesus give us the Eucharist?*

Jesus blessed the bread, broke it, and gave it to His apostles, saying, "Take this, all of you, and eat it. This is My Body." He took the cup of wine, blessed it and gave it to them, saying, "Take this, all of you, and drink from it. This is the cup of My Blood."

*61. How does Jesus' action continue today?*

The sacrament of the Holy Eucharist takes place in the Mass when the priest blesses the bread and wine and prays the blessing of Jesus.

*62. What is the Mass?*

The Mass is the sacrifice of Jesus on the Cross, extended through time and space. Through the Mass, the sacrifice offered once and for all on the Cross is made ever present.

*63. What happens to the bread and wine?*

When the priest blesses these gifts, the bread and wine become the Body and Blood of Jesus. We call this the Real Presence. The change that takes place is called transubstantiation.

*64. How long is Jesus present in the sacrament?*

Jesus remains present in the Eucharist, even after the Mass, when the sacrament is ordinarily kept in a special place called the tabernacle.

*65. Why did Jesus give us the sacrament of Holy Eucharist?*

He gave us the sacrament so that we could be deeply united with Him and His Church, to increase His grace within us, and to strengthen us in our struggle against sin.

*66. How do we receive the Holy Eucharist?*

We receive the Body and Blood of Jesus at Holy Communion, normally during the Mass.

*67. How should we prepare to receive Holy Communion?*

We should keep Jesus in mind, and we should speak to Him in prayer. Above all, we should be in the state of grace. The best way to stay in the state of grace is by going regularly to the sacrament of penance. Also, we must fast for an hour before receiving Holy Communion.

*68. What is required by the Communion fast?*
We must go without food or drink for one hour. Water or medicine never breaks the fast.

*69. Who celebrates the sacrament of the Holy Eucharist?*
Only an ordained priest can consecrate the bread and wine so that they become the Body and Blood of Jesus.

*70. How often may we receive Holy Communion?*
We should receive Holy Communion as often as we can, even every day. We may receive Holy Communion no more than twice in a single day.

*71. Why is the Eucharist so important?*
The Holy Eucharist is the fullness of our sharing in the life of Jesus. It sums up our entire Faith. It is the source of God's grace for the Christian today. It is the presence of God among us.

*72. What is the sacrament of penance?*
It is the sacrament through which God forgives our sins and reconciles us with Himself and His Church.

*73. What are other names for the sacrament of penance?*
The sacrament of penance is also called the sacrament of reconciliation, the sacrament of forgiveness, the sacrament of confession, and the sacrament of conversion.

*74. When did Jesus give us the sacrament of penance?*

Jesus gave the authority to forgive sins to the apostles, when He said, "I will give you the keys of the kingdom of heaven, and whatever you bind on earth will be bound in heaven, and whatever you loose on earth will be loosed in heaven." This power continues today through the ministry of the bishops and priests who follow in the footsteps of the apostles.

*75. How do priests give us God's forgiveness?*
They forgive sins, in the name of Jesus Christ, through the prayer of absolution.

*76. Why do we need the sacrament of penance?*
Because all of us sin, and the Bible says that even the best people sin every day. Our sins are offenses against God, and only God can forgive sins.

*77. What makes a good confession?*
Penance requires that we be sorry for our sins, that we confess them to a priest, and that we complete the penance assigned to us by the priest.

*78. How often should we go to confession?*
If we have committed a mortal sin, we should go immediately. But we should also make a habit of frequent confession of ordinary (venial) sins.

*79. Why should we go to penance so often?*
Frequent confession of venial sins helps us to form our conscience, to overcome habits of sin, and to grow in holiness.

*80. How should we prepare for confession?*

The best way to prepare for confession is by making a daily examination of conscience.

*81. What is an examination of conscience?*

The examination of conscience is a prayerful look at our actions, thoughts, and words in a given day, to determine how faithful we have been to the commandments of God.

*82. What is the sacrament of anointing of the sick?*

It is the sacrament that brings healing, comfort, and strength, through the grace of the Holy Spirit, to those who are sick or elderly.

*83. Why should the sick be anointed?*
Jesus showed constant care for sick people. In the Bible, we read that St. James the apostle wrote to the early Church: "Is anyone among you sick? Let him call for the priests and let them pray over him, anointing him with oil."

*84. How is the sacrament of anointing celebrated?*
An ordained priest lays his hands on the sick person, prays, and anoints the person with oil.

*85. Who should receive the anointing of the sick?*
Ordinarily, the sacrament is received by people who are seriously ill, in danger of death, or people who are very old.

*86. What does the sick person receive in the sacrament of anointing?*

The sick person receives grace to be strong in facing illness. The sick person receives the forgiveness of sins. Sometimes, the person also receives healing of the illness.

*87. What is the sacrament of holy orders?*
Holy orders is the sacrament by which bishops, priests, and deacons are ordained to carry on the mission of Jesus and His apostles.

*88. When did Jesus establish holy orders?*
Jesus established the priesthood of His new covenant at the Last Supper, on Holy Thursday, when He instituted the Eucharist and told His apostles, "Do this in memory of Me."

*89. Who can receive holy orders?*
The Church gives the sacrament of holy
orders to baptized men who have been
called by God and who have been
judged ready for ministry to the
Church.

*90. How is the sacrament administered?*
The bishop administers the sacrament
by laying his hands on the man and
praying over him.

*91. How is a man changed by holy orders?*
Ordination gives a man an indelible
spiritual mark. This mark is permanent.
Once ordained, a man is a priest forever. In celebrating the sacraments, a
priest acts in the person of Jesus Christ.

*92. What are the primary works of the priest?*

Priests are ordained to serve the people of God, by teaching them, guiding them, and sanctifying them.

*93. What is the sacrament of marriage?*

Marriage is the sacrament that brings together a man and a woman in a holy and lifelong bond, so that, as a couple, they can grow closer to each other and to God, and bring children into the world.

*94. Who can receive the sacrament of marriage?*

A baptized man and a baptized woman who are prepared and are free to make such a commitment.

*95. Who are the ministers of the sacrament?*

The ministers of marriage are the man and woman.

*96. When does the sacrament take place?*

The sacrament takes place, in the Church, when the man and woman freely exchange their consent to be married. The priest receives their consent and gives the blessing of the Church.

*97. What is required of the man and woman who are married?*

They must love one another totally, for the rest of their lives, and be open to children as a gift from God.

*98. What is a sacramental?*
A sacramental is any action or thing blessed by the Church to inspire Christians to prayer and love of God. These include the Sign of the Cross, holy water, prayers of blessing, works of art, rosaries, candles, blessed ashes, blessed palms, medals, and scapulars.

*99. What do sacramentals do?*
They prepare the heart and mind to be more open to grace. They do not convey God's grace as sacraments do.

# _PART THREE

# THE MORAL LIFE

*100. What must we do to gain God's promise of salvation and happiness?*
We must follow the way of Christ by loving God and neighbor and following the commandments. This is called the moral life.

*101. How did Jesus sum up this moral life?*
Jesus said that the greatest commandment is to love God with all your heart, soul, and mind, and to love your neighbor as yourself.

*102. What are the commandments of God?*

On Mount Sinai, God gave Moses Ten Commandments:

1. I am the Lord your God: you shall not have strange Gods before Me.
2. You shall not take the name of the LORD your God in vain.
3. Remember to keep holy the LORD's day.
4. Honor your father and your mother.
5. You shall not kill.
6. You shall not commit adultery.
7. You shall not steal.
8. You shall not bear false witness against your neighbor.
9. You shall not covet your neighbor's wife.
10. You shall not covet your neighbor's goods.

(The Traditional Catechetical Formula, from the *Catechism of the Catholic Church.*)

### 103. What does the first commandment require?

The first commandment teaches us to love God with all our heart, mind, and soul. This commandment requires our total loyalty to the one true Faith and forbids us to make anything else more important than God in our lives.

### 104. How do we give honor to God?

We adore God by praying to Him, offering Him fitting worship, and keeping to the way of life He gave us.

### 105. How can the first commandment be broken?

The first commandment can be broken by turning away from the Catholic Faith, by putting other things before God in our lives, or by believing in superstition, magic, or false religion.

*106. What does the second commandment require?*

We must honor the name of God by speaking of Him reverently and not using His name in a disrespectful way.

*107. How can the second commandment be broken?*

We can abuse God's name by speaking badly of Him, by failing to show respect for His name, by referring to Him with hatred or defiance, by using His name to curse people. This commandment also forbids us to swear falsely by God's name.

*108. What does the third commandment teach?*

The third commandment calls us to keep holy the Lord's day, Sunday.

*109. How do we keep Sunday holy?*
We keep Sunday holy first of all by
going to Mass, which we are required
to do by our Catholic Faith.

*110. How else do we keep Sunday
holy?*
We keep the day holy by resting from
work, doing good deeds, and spending
time reading the Bible and praying.

*111. What does the third commandment
forbid?*
The third commandment forbids us to
do work that is unnecessary and keeps
our minds and hearts from the worship
due to God. We should also avoid making others do such work.

*112. What else does the third com-
mandment require?*
The third commandment requires us to

attend Mass on holy days of obligation, and to treat those special days as we would treat a Sunday.

*113. What does the fourth commandment teach?*
The fourth commandment tells us to honor our parents.

*114. How do we honor our parents?*
We honor our parents by loving, respecting, and obeying them, and by helping them to keep a bright and cheerful home and to build a strong family.

*115. Why do we work to build a strong family?*
The family is the building block of society, and every home is a Church, a holy place that reflects the love of God.

*116. Does the requirement extend beyond honor for our parents?*
Yes, the fourth commandment requires that we give obedience to all rightful authority in family, Church, and state.

*117. What are the sins against the fourth commandment?*
People break the fourth commandment by being selfish and unforgiving toward family members, irresponsible in fulfilling their duties at home, and disobedient or disrespectful to their elders.

*118. What does the fifth commandment teach?*
The fifth commandment teaches us not to kill.

*119. Why does God command us not to kill?*

God commands us not to kill because human life is sacred, from its beginning to its end. Human life is made in God's image. No one, under any circumstances, may destroy an innocent human life.

*120. How can we best fulfill the fifth commandment?*
We fulfill the fifth commandment by living in peace with all our neighbors, by respecting their rights, and by taking proper care of ourselves and others.

*121. What is forbidden by the fifth commandment?*
Murder, abortion, euthanasia, suicide, and abuse of our bodies are the gravest offenses against the fifth commandment.

*122. Does the fifth commandment forbid anything else?*
Jesus said that the commandment also forbids anger, revenge, hatred, and fighting.

*123. What does the sixth commandment teach?*
The sixth commandment teaches that people should not commit adultery.

*124. What does the sixth commandment require?*
The sixth commandment requires us to be pure, chaste, and modest, and to be faithful to the vocation God has given us.

*125. What is chastity?*
Chastity is the virtue that enables us to take charge of our body's passions and desires and keep them in line with God's will. To be chaste, one must pray.

*126. What is modesty?*

Modesty means respecting the privacy of intimate details of everyone's life. This is shown by the way we talk, dress, act, and even the way we look at one another.

*127. What are the sins against the sixth commandment?*

The sixth commandment forbids using any actions outside of marriage that belong only in marriage, such as the signs of affection between a husband and wife. The sixth commandment forbids us to violate another person's privacy by our looks or actions. The sixth commandment also forbids us to view immodest or indecent books, movies, or television programs.

*128. What does the seventh command-
ment teach?*

The seventh commandment teaches us
not to steal.

*129. What does the seventh command-
ment require?*

The seventh commandment asks us to
live in charity with our neighbors,
showing respect for the people and the
goods of the earth and sharing them
justly.

*130. Does the seventh commandment
require anything more?*

Jesus said we have a special duty to
care for the poor through acts of kindness and mercy.

*131. How are we to live in charity with
our neighbors?*

The seventh commandment calls us to

respect their property and pay whatever we owe.

*132. What does the seventh commandment forbid?*
The seventh commandment forbids stealing, withholding money or things that rightly belong to someone else, and selfishly refusing to share our goods.

*133. What does the eighth commandment teach?*
The eighth commandment teaches us to tell the truth at all times.

*134. What does the eighth commandment forbid?*
The eighth commandment forbids us to tell lies, spread gossip, ruin another's reputation, exaggerate, boast, or hold back information that should be told.

*135. What does the ninth commandment teach?*

The ninth commandment teaches us to keep our thoughts pure.

*136. What does the ninth commandment forbid?*

The ninth commandment forbids unchaste thoughts and desires that go against faithfulness to one's vocation.

*137. How do we remain pure in our thoughts?*

Purity of heart requires modesty in dress and speech. Purity comes from living a chaste and prayerful life.

*138. What does the tenth commandment teach?*

The tenth commandment teaches us to be satisfied with what we have and to be grateful to God.

*139. What does the tenth command-*
*ment forbid?*
The tenth commandment forbids us to
be jealous of others, their qualities, or
their possessions.

*140. What are the sins against the tenth*
*commandment?*
The sins against the tenth commandment are greed and envy.

*141. Why should Christians obey the*
*commandments of God?*
So that they can live in freedom and
gain the salvation that Christ won for
everyone.

*142. What are the precepts of the*
*Church?*
The precepts of the Church are the du-
ties of every Catholic. They are:

1. Go to Mass on Sundays and holy days of obligation.
2. Receive Holy Communion and confession regularly.
3. Study Catholic teaching.
4. Observe the marriage laws of the Church.
5. Support the Church financially.
6. Observe the prescribed days for fasting and abstinence.
7. Join in the missionary work of the Church.

*143. How do we live in freedom?*
We are truly free when we choose to do what is right, what God wants us to do. We lose our freedom when we choose to break the commandments and do evil.

*144. How do we protect our freedom?*
We protect our freedom by forming the

conscience that God gave us. A well-formed conscience is God's voice speaking in our hearts, helping us to do good.

*145. How do we form our conscience?*
We form our conscience by praying, reading the Scriptures, receiving the sacraments, following the advice of our parents and priests, and knowing the teachings of the Church.

*146. What is the surest way we can continue on the way of Christ, even when it is difficult?*
The surest way we can continue on the way of Christ is by forming good habits of mind, heart, and action. These habits are called virtues.

*147. What are the most important virtues?*

The most important virtues are those given to us by God, called the "theological virtues." They are faith, hope, and charity.

*148. What are the most important human virtues?*

The most important human virtues are prudence (or sound judgment), justice, fortitude (bravery and strength), and temperance (self-control).

*149. What are the works of mercy?*

The works of mercy are charitable deeds by which we help our neighbor. They are usually divided into "corporal" and "spiritual" works.

*150. What are the corporal works of mercy?*

The corporal works of mercy are: feeding the hungry, sheltering the homeless, clothing the naked, visiting the sick, and burying the dead.

*151. What are the spiritual works of mercy?*
The spiritual works of mercy are: instructing the ignorant, advising the doubtful, correcting the sinner, comforting the afflicted, forgiving wrongs, bearing wrongs patiently, and praying for the living and the dead.

# PART FOUR

## PRAYER

*152. What is prayer?*
Prayer is raising one's heart and mind to God, and asking good things of God. Prayer is talking with God.

*153. When should we pray?*
The Bible says we should pray always, meaning that we should be aware of God's presence at all times. But we also need to set special times when we can be alone with God.

*154. What are the best times for special prayer?*

It is important that we set time aside for prayer at the beginning and end of each day. Sunday and holy days are times the Church marks especially for prayer.

*155. What makes good prayer?*
When we pray well, we are attentive to God, we trust in Him and His grace, and we continue even when we find prayer difficult.

*156. Who helps us to pray?*
Jesus gave us the Holy Spirit to help us in our prayer. The Holy Spirit also works through the Church to help us to pray.

*157. What are the different kinds of prayer?*
There are five main kinds of prayer: adoration, which honors God for His

goodness and majesty; petition, which asks things of God; intercession, which we offer for the good of other people; contrition, which shows our sorrow for our sins; and thanksgiving, which shows our gratitude.

*158. How did Jesus say we should pray?*
Jesus gave us a model for prayer by His life of prayer. He gave us a perfect prayer in the Our Father.

*159. Why is the Our Father the perfect prayer?*
The Our Father sums up the whole Gospel. It tells of our dependence on God, our trust in His goodness, and our desire to do His will and live with Him forever.

*160. What other prayers does the Church recommend?*

The Sign of the Cross, the Hail Mary, the Glory Be, the Apostles' Creed, the Acts of Faith, Hope, and Love, the Act of Contrition, and the Rosary are the most commonly used prayers in the Church. There are many others that can help us to pray well.

# A TREASURY OF PRAYERS

## THE SIGN OF THE CROSS

In the name of the Father, and of the Son, and of the Holy Spirit. Amen.

## THE OUR FATHER

Our Father, who art in heaven,
hallowed be Thy name.
Thy kingdom come.
Thy will be done on earth as it is in heaven.
Give us this day our daily bread.
And forgive us our trespasses
as we forgive those who trespass against us.
And lead us not into temptation,
but deliver us from evil. Amen.

# THE HAIL MARY

Hail Mary, full of grace,
the Lord is with you.
Blessed are you among women,
and blessed is the fruit of your womb,
Jesus.
Holy Mary, Mother of God,
pray for us sinners
now and at the hour of our death.
Amen.

# THE GLORY BE

Glory be to the Father,
and to the Son,
and to the Holy Spirit.
As it was in the beginning,
is now, and will be forever. Amen.

# ACT OF CONTRITION

O my God, I am heartily sorry
for having offended You,
and I detest all my sins

because of Your just punishments,
but most of all because they offend You,
my God,
who are all good and deserving of all
my love.
I firmly resolve, with the help of Your
grace,
to sin no more and to avoid the near
occasions of sin. Amen.

## GRACE AT MEALS

*Before the meal:*
Bless us, O Lord, and these Your gifts,
which we are about to receive from
Your bounty, through Christ Our Lord.
Amen.

*After the meal:*
We give You thanks, almighty God, for
these and all Your gifts, which we have
received from Your bounty through
Christ Our Lord. Amen.

# Hail Holy Queen

Hail Holy Queen, mother of mercy,
our life, our sweetness, and our hope,
to you do we cry, poor banished children of Eve;
to you do we send up our sighs,
mourning and weeping in this valley of tears.
Turn, then, O most gracious advocate,
your eyes of mercy toward us,
and after this our exile
show to us the blessed fruit of your womb, Jesus.
O clement, O loving, O sweet Virgin Mary.
Pray for us, O holy Mother of God,
that we may be made worthy of the promises of Christ.

# THE ROSARY

1. Begin with the Sign of the Cross.
2. Holding the Cross at the end of the beads, pray the Apostles' Creed.
3. On the first bead, pray the Our Father.
4. On the next three beads, pray Hail Marys. Then pray a Glory Be.
5. The rest of the beads follow a pattern: one bead by itself, followed by ten beads together. On the bead by itself pray an Our Father. On each of the ten beads, pray a Hail Mary.
5. Each set of ten beads is called a "decade." On each decade, we remember one of the events in the lives of Jesus and Mary. Try to picture that event, and talk to Jesus about it in your heart.
6. End each decade with a Glory Be.
7. At the end of all the beads, pray the Hail Holy Queen.

# THE MYSTERIES OF THE ROSARY

*The Joyful Mysteries (prayed Mondays and Thursdays)*

1. The Annunciation
2. The Visitation
3. The Birth of Jesus
4. The Presentation of Jesus in the Temple
5. The Finding of Jesus in the Temple

*The Sorrowful Mysteries (prayed Tuesdays and Fridays)*

1. The Agony in the Garden
2. The Scourging at the Pillar
3. The Crowning With Thorns
4. The Carrying of the Cross
5. The Crucifixion and Death

*The Glorious Mysteries (prayed Wednesdays, Saturdays, and Sundays)*

1. The Resurrection
2. The Ascension

3. The Descent of the Holy Spirit Upon the Apostles
4. The Assumption of Mary Into Heaven
5. The Crowning of Mary in Heaven

## ACT OF FAITH

O my God, I firmly believe that You are one God in three divine Persons: Father, Son, and Holy Spirit. I believe that Your divine Son became man and died for our sins, and that He will come to judge the living and the dead. I believe these and all the truths which the holy Catholic Church teaches, because You have revealed them, who can neither deceive nor be deceived. In this faith I desire to live and die. Amen.

## ACT OF HOPE

O my God, trusting in Your promises and the infinite merits of Jesus Christ, our Redeemer, I hope for the pardon of my sins and the graces I need to serve You faithfully on earth, and to obtain eternal life in heaven. Amen

## ACT OF LOVE

O my God, I love You above all things, with my whole heart and soul, because You are infinitely good and deserving of all my love. I love my neighbor as myself for love of You. Amen.

## PRAYER TO THE HOLY SPIRIT

Come, Holy Spirit, fill the hearts of Your faithful and enkindle in them the fire of Your divine love. Send forth Your Spirit and they shall be created, and You shall renew the face of the earth. O God, who instructs the hearts of the faithful by the light of the Holy Spirit, grant us by the same Spirit to be truly wise and ever to rejoice in His consolations. Amen.

## PRAYER AT MIDDAY
### (THE ANGELUS)

The angel of the Lord declared unto Mary.

And she conceived by the Holy Spirit.

*Hail Mary, full of grace . . .*

Behold the handmaid of the Lord.

Let it be done to me according to Your word.

*Hail Mary, full of grace . . .*

And the Word was made flesh.

And dwelt among us.

*Hail Mary, full of grace . . .*

Pray for us, O holy Mother of God.

That we may be made worthy of the promises of Christ.

Let us pray. Pour forth, we beseech You, O Lord, Your grace into our hearts, that we to whom the Incarnation of Christ, Your Son, was made known by the message of an angel, may by His passion and Cross be brought to the glory of His resurrection, through the same Christ our Lord. Amen.

## EASTER SEASON PRAYER AT MIDDAY (THE REGINA CAELI)

O Queen of heaven, rejoice! Alleluia!
For He whom you merited to bear!
Alleluia!
Has risen as He said! Alleluia!
Pray for us to God! Alleluia!
Rejoice and be glad, O Virgin Mary!
Alleluia!
For the Lord has risen indeed! Alleluia!
O God, who through the resurrection of Your Son, Our Lord Jesus Christ, willed to fill the world with joy, grant, we beseech You, that through His Virgin Mother, Mary, we may come to the joys of everlasting life, through the same Christ Our Lord. Amen.

# HOLY DAYS OF OBLIGATION IN THE UNITED STATES

Mary, Mother of God, January 1

The Ascension, 40 days after Easter

Assumption of the Blessed Virgin Mary, August 15

All Saints, November 1

Immaculate Conception, December 8

Christmas Day, December 25

# A Closer Look at the Mass

*Where are you* when you go to Mass? If you could see things as they are, if you could see the Mass in all its spiritual reality, you would see that you are at Calvary. Jesus' sacrifice took place once for all time and for each person who would live down through the ages. Yet He desired that *you* should be there. So, on the night before He suffered, He instituted the Mass, to extend His one sacrifice specifically to you and your parish community.

The Mass is communal, but it is also personal. You stand before the altar with your neighbors, friends, the local merchants, and folks who are just passing through town. All together, you are the Body of Christ on earth. Yet Christ draws you alone — and each of those beside you, alone in love — to spend some time apart with Him in the Mass. You are there with Him at Calvary. You are caught up in His Paschal Mystery.

And, yes, you are joined by your fellow parishioners. But open your eyes: You are also joined by hosts of angels, and by Christians all around the world and down through the ages, the millions of unknown saints from all salvation history.

Open your eyes to see the fulfillment of His promise: "I am the living bread which came down from heaven; if any one eats of this bread, he will live forever" (John 6:51).

◆◆◆◆◆

The English word "Mass" comes from the concluding words of the Latin liturgy, "*Ite, missa est,*" which is popularly translated as "Go, it is ended." The ancient Church called the Mass by many words: "Eucharist" (or "thanksgiving"), "liturgy" (or "work of the people"), and the "Passion of the Lord."

The first Mass was the Last Supper. With His farewell to His friends, Jesus ensured that He would remain with them always — really present — His Body, Blood, Soul, and Divinity. That night, He established the Eucharist as He blessed the bread and broke it, and He established the priesthood so that the Eucharist could be offered for Christians of every age. He told His apostles, His first priests, "Do this . . . in remembrance of Me" (1 Corinthians 11:25).

After His resurrection, His urgent desire was for communion with His friends. That first Easter Sunday, after nightfall in the village of Emmaus, His disciples "knew Him," St. Luke tells us, "in the breaking of the bread" (24:35). So, too, do we know Him today.

The apostles continued the celebration of the Mass after Jesus' Ascension. Among the first snapshots we have of the first Christians is the assurance that "they devoted themselves . . . to the breaking of the bread and to the prayers" (Acts 2:42).

As the Church grew, St. Paul outlined a profound theology of the Eucharist as memorial and sacrifice. "For as often as you eat this bread and drink the cup, you proclaim the death of the Lord until He comes" (1 Corinthians 11:26). You should read all of that eleventh chapter of First Corinthians.

Outside the New Testament, the oldest surviving Church document is *The Didache*, probably from the late first century. Among its aims is to give clear instruction on the conduct of the liturgy. The prayers appear to be published in sequence, culminating in the call to Communion: "If anyone is holy, let him advance. If anyone is not, let him be converted."

Just a few years later, about A.D. 100, St. Ignatius of Antioch outlined the requirements for a valid liturgy and noted that already there were heretics who denied the Real Presence: "From the Eucharist and prayer they hold aloof, because they do not confess that the Eucharist is the flesh of our Savior Jesus Christ."

St. Justin in 155, writing to a pagan audience, described the Christian liturgy in details recognizable to anyone who attends a Mass today, concluding, "the food that has been made the Eucharist by the prayer of His word, and which nourishes our flesh and blood by assimilation, is both the flesh and blood of that Jesus who was made flesh." (Read Justin's description in *The Catechism of the Catholic Church*, no. 1345.)

❖❖❖❖❖

Who offers the Mass? Jesus Christ is both priest and victim. St. Augustine said, "Christ is the one who offers; He is also the offering." His sacrifice recalls the sacrifices of the Old Testament: of Abel and Abraham, of Melchisedech, priest of Salem, and of the Temple liturgy. The ordained priest offers the Mass "in the person of Christ." Tradition refers to the priest as "another Christ."

Yet we are a nation of priests, and all believers have some share in the priesthood of Christ (see 1 Peter 2:5). Pope John Paul II wrote of the laity that "their work, prayers and apostolic endeavors, their ordinary married and family life, their daily labor, their mental and physical relaxation . . . all of these become spiritual sacrifices acceptable to God through Jesus Christ. During the celebration of the Eucharist, these sacrifices are most lovingly offered to the Father along with the Lord's Body. Thus as worshipers whose every deed is holy, the lay faithful consecrate the world itself to God."

❖❖❖❖❖

We open the Mass with the Sign of the Cross, the most ancient blessing of the Church (see Matthew 28:19). And we see that the Mass is a Trinitarian prayer. We beseech the Father to send us the Son by the power of the Holy Spirit.

As the priest says, "The Lord be with you," he acknowledges the promise of Jesus — that wherever two or more are gathered in His name, there He is in their midst.

Then follows the Penitential Rite. *The Didache*, like St. Paul (1 Corinthians 11:28-31), requires confession of sins before a believer may approach the sacrament. With the prayers "Lord, have mercy" and "I confess . . . ," we try to see ourselves as we are, so that we might more clearly see Jesus as He is. The "Lord, have mercy" was originally a longer litany of supplication. A Spanish pilgrim wrote of hearing the Kyrie in the liturgy in Jerusalem about A.D. 500.

If in the Penitential Rite we see ourselves as we are, in the Gloria we proclaim God as He is. The Church used this enthusiastic prayer as early as the second century. It celebrates the glory of God in His Incarnation as Jesus Christ. Its opening lines come from the angels' song in Luke's Christmas story.

Then begins the Liturgy of the Word, the "readings." "Faith comes by hearing," St. Paul says in Romans 10:17. And so we receive the words of the Bible, as the earliest Christians did, from the Church. The first reading is usually from the Old Testament, followed by a responsory from the psalms of King David. The Second reading usually comes from a New Testament letter. And the Liturgy of the Word culminates in the proclamation of the Gospel, with a story from the life and teaching of Jesus. We listen attentively, preparing ourselves by tracing a cross on our forehead that we may understand the Gospel, on our lips that we may proclaim it, and on our heart that we may love it. The Gospel is preceded by a Hebrew shout of joy: Alleluia!

In the homily, the Holy Spirit works through the priest, who guides, exhorts, and teaches the congregation, drawing wisdom from the Scriptures.

The Creed is a profession of the basic truths of Faith. Faith is not merely, or primarily, a subjective feeling. It is our personal response to objective Truth — the reality of God, the Trinity and Incarnation, the Person of Jesus, and the mission of His Church.

The prayers of petition bring the Liturgy of the Word to a close. At this point, in the early Church, all those who were not yet baptized were dismissed from the assembly. The uninitiated were unprepared to enter the mysteries of the Eucharist.

❖❖❖❖❖

With the Liturgy of the Eucharist, a "new Mass" begins with the words we heard at the start of the Mass: "The Lord be with you."

In the offertory, we bring our gifts to the altar to be transformed by Christ. Remember that Pope John Paul says that with the bread and wine, we bring our work, our prayer, our life. St. Ignatius of Antioch imagined himself, in his martyrdom, to be an offering of wheat to be ground down by the teeth of the lions. The Mass is a sacrifice, and we share in that sacrifice. Our Faith requires self-offering, self-dying, and rising.

The bread and wine we offer suggests many motifs from the Bible. In the West, since the ninth century, we have used unleavened bread made of wheat flour with no admixtures. The bread, the Host, evokes the manna that rained from heaven as the Israelites were delivered from slavery in Egypt. We too receive our deliverance and our bread from heaven. The wine recalls the Passover Seder meal, as well as the offering of Melchisedech in the Book of Genesis.

The priest pours wine and a small amount of water into the chalice. The prayer at this time makes clear that his action symbolizes the union of Christ's humanity and divinity, as well as our participation in that mystery: "May we come to share in the divinity of Christ, who humbled Himself to share in our humanity." The water and wine also symbolize the blood and water that flowed from Jesus' wounded side. And they are said to symbolize our good works, the small portion of water representing our share, while the greater portion of wine stands for God's grace.

The washing of the priest's hands is symbolic of the purifying of the soul. And then, purified, we stand at heaven's gate. With the "Holy, Holy, Holy," we join our prayer to the hymn of the angels (see Revelation 4:2-11 and Isaiah 6:1-3).

More than a millennium ago, St. John of Damascus wrote, "If I am asked how bread is changed into the Body of Christ, I answer: 'The Holy Ghost overshadows the priest and operates in the same manner in the elements which He effected in the womb of the Virgin Mary.' "

And that is exactly what happens in the course of the Eucharistic Prayer. It is a profound prayer of thanksgiving that includes the remembrance of the whole Church and a retelling of the story of salvation. The words of the Eucharistic Prayer always recall us to the room of the Last Supper.

At the words of institution — "This is My Body . . . This is the cup of My Blood" — the gifts are definitively and substantially changed. On the altar, there is no longer a crumb we can call bread or a drop we can call wine. The elements have become the Body and Blood of Jesus Christ.

And then, as Paul predicted, we proclaim "the death of the Lord" in the mystery of faith.

At the end of the Eucharistic Prayer, the priest intones: "Through Him, with Him, in Him . . ." And, with our Great Amen, we join all creation in praising the Holy Trinity for ever.

With the Our Father, we join Christians of every age in praying the perfect prayer, the words Jesus Himself gave us.

The priest, then, breaks the Host, again reminds us of the Last Supper. This action symbolizes the Body of Christ broken in the Passion, but also the sacrament of Christ distributed to the many.

The next prayer, the Lamb of God, is probably a remnant of a longer litany to Jesus first used in the East. Now we recall Jesus as our Passover lamb (see John 1:36). Our prayer shows that the New Covenant continues and fulfills the Old. A Syrian pope, Sergius I, established the Lamb of God in the Roman liturgy in the seventh century.

The Sign of Peace is a practice of the ancient Church restored to the liturgy in recent years. It is a sign of the Church's communion in Christ. It is also a fulfillment of Jesus' command that we make peace with our neighbor before approaching the altar (see Matthew 5:24).

Then comes a dramatic moment. In the course of the Mass, we have seen ourselves as we are (the Penitential Rite), and we have proclaimed God as He is (the Gloria, Creed, and the Great Amen). We can see clearly that we are sinners and He is God. So when the priest elevates the Host this last time before Communion, we pray the centurion's prayer: "Lord, I am not worthy to receive You, but only say the word . . ." (see Matthew 8:8).

Then we rise, make some act of reverence before the Host and, when the priest utters the mystery, "The Body of Christ," we profess our belief: "Amen." And we take Our Lord in Holy Communion.

Then, almost hurriedly, it seems, we

are dismissed, sent on our way with a blessing. "The Mass is ended. Go in peace."

We have to take our Lord out into the world. The Mass has to reach out into our day, just as we must raise our every day to the altar.

# WHAT IS THE SACRAMENT OF RECONCILIATION?

First of all, it is a *sacrament*: an outward sign, instituted by Jesus and entrusted to the Church, to dispense divine life to us. The *Catechism of the Catholic Church* gives us five names by which the sacrament is known: the sacrament of conversion, the sacrament of penance, the sacrament of confession, the sacrament of forgiveness, and the sacrament of reconciliation (*Catechism of the Catholic Church*, nos. 1423-1424).

Jesus gave us the sacrament when He breathed His Spirit on the apostles

(His first priests) and declared to them that "Whose sins you forgive are forgiven them. . ." (John 20:23).

That is good news to all of us, because we are all sinners. "If we say 'We are without sin,' we deceive ourselves, and the truth is not in us" (1 John 1:8). We know we are in need of forgiveness — for the bad things we've thought, said, and done — yet we ourselves are not very good at forgiving. Jesus knew this, and so He gave us a way that we could be assured of perfect forgiveness — God's forgiveness.

In the sacrament of reconciliation, we confess our sins to God through His minister, the priest. The priest absolves us "on behalf of Christ" *(Catechism of the Catholic Church*, no. 1442). Some people say they do not go to confession because they would rather "eliminate the middleman" and confess directly to God. But we must keep in mind that God Himself willed that we take advantage of sacramental confession. And we can discern many reasons why this is a wise course for us.

First, because anyone who has ever gone to confession knows that there is a world of difference between *thinking* about a sin and *speaking* about it — aloud — before another person. In confession, God helps us to confront our sins in a profound way, by speaking their name while another person listens.

That is humbling.

But it is also healing, because, in doing so, we reconcile ourselves, first of all, with God, who is all good and who desires our repentance. We also "make up" with the Church, in the person of the priest, because the Church too is wounded by our sins.

The Church, then, can dispense the

healing of Christ when the priest pronounces the words of absolution. Sometimes, the priest might also offer advice to help us overcome sinful habits and avoid temptations in the future. By the grace and good counsel of the sacrament, then, each of us can become a little bit more like the person God created us to be. We can grow in wholeness, happiness, and holiness. And we will grow in ways that we just could not grow before absolution, because sin is the most severe disability a person can know, and confession really heals us.

The healing that takes place when we confess is primarily spiritual, though it works in a way that is similar to physical healing. When we get stitches or take an antibiotic, we might know that we have been cured — and tests can confirm the result — yet, perhaps for weeks afterward, we still feel the effects of our illness or injury. In the same way, even after confession, we have to live with the effects of our sins and do what we can to remedy the situations we have damaged. And we have to stay faithful to a program of "rehabilitation" — through prayer, sacraments, and the cultivation of virtue — so that we will avoid committing the same sins in the future. Our confessor can be a great help in working out such a program, especially if we make it a point to see him regularly (once a month or so).

An important part of our healing is the penance the priest asks us to perform in reparation for our sins. It is not that our work could ever make up for our breaches with God, who is all-good. It cannot. But, by offering some small prayer or work of mercy, we unite ourselves with Jesus Christ, whose work and prayer made perfect satisfaction for our sins. According to the *Catechism*, "such penances help configure us to Christ" (no. 1460). They make us more like Him.

If we are honest with ourselves, we know that we could use a good dose of Christ's life in our own everyday lives. By ourselves, we can make a mess of things; and when we inevitably do, we ache for the forgiveness that only God can give.

He gives it freely through the confessional.

# How to Make a Good Confession

Confession is not a difficult matter, but it does require some preparation. As with all things, we should begin with prayer, placing ourselves in the presence of God. Then we should try to review our lives since our last confession, searching out our thoughts, words, and actions that did not conform to God's love, to His law, or to the laws of the Church. Reviewing our life this way is called an "examination of conscience," and it is a good practice for every day of our lives (see page 103).

We should not let too much time pass between our visits to the sacrament of reconciliation. The Church asks us to go at least once a year, but suggests that we go regularly, perhaps once a month. If we go more often, we can more often receive the graces to improve our lives.

Once you are there for the sacrament, follow these four steps to a good confession:

1. **Tell all.** Try not to leave any serious sins out. Start with the one that is toughest to say.
2. **Be clear.** Try not to be subtle or euphemistic.
3. **Be sorry.** Remember, it is God you have offended, and His forgiveness you seek.
4. **Be brief.** No need to go into detail. Often when we do, we are just trying to excuse ourselves.

If you have not been to confession in a while, this is not a reason to worry.

The Church loves to welcome prodigal children home. But please do not delay any longer — just go. You might even want to make an appointment with your parish priest so you can spend a little more time without worrying about delaying others who might be waiting in line. Let the priest know at the start that it has been a while since your last confession, and that you are not sure how to proceed. And if you are nervous, say so. The point of the sacrament is repentance and mercy; so the more mercy the priest can dispense in the name of God, the more joyous the occasion should be.

# The Rite of Reconciliation

After the customary greetings, the penitent crosses himself.

*In the name of the Father, and of the Son, and of the Holy Spirit, Amen.*

The priest urges the penitent to have confidence in God. The priest may say:

*May the Lord be in your heart and help you to confess your sins with true sorrow.*

Either the priest or the penitent may read or say by heart some words taken from the Holy Scripture about the mercy of God and repentance, e.g.

*Lord, You know all things; You know that I love You* (John 21:17).

The penitent accuses himself of his sins. The priest gives opportune advice, imposes the penance on him, and invites the penitent to manifest his contrition. The penitent may say, for example,

*Lord Jesus, Son of God, have mercy on me, a sinner.*

The priest gives absolution:

*God, the Father of mercies, through the death and resurrection of His Son has reconciled the world to Himself and sent His Holy Spirit among us for the forgiveness of sins; through the ministry of the Church, may God give you pardon and peace, and I absolve you*

*from your sins in the name of the Father, and of the Son, and the of the Holy Spirit.*

The penitent answers: *Amen.*

The priest dismisses the penitent with this prayer or one like it:

*May the Passion of Our Lord Jesus Christ, the intercession of the Blessed Virgin Mary and of all the saints, whatever good you do and suffering you endure heal your sins, help you to grow in holiness, and reward you with eternal life. Go in peace.*

The penitent should fulfill the penance imposed without delay.

# How to Make an Examination of Conscience

In an examination of conscience, we try to see our day as God sees it. It is a review of our day's events, measuring our thoughts, words, and deeds against the moral law and the demands of the Christian vocation. The practice enables us to see our faults and root them out with God's help.

To make an examination of conscience, we should:

1. Begin by recalling that we are in God's presence.
2. Consider our day's events, referring

to questions we have prepared. (For examples, see below.)

3. Tell God we are sorry for our sins.

4. Make a firm resolution not to sin again.

## SOME SUGGESTED QUESTIONS

Do I pray to God every day? Do I pray for my family and friends?

Have I thanked God for His gifts to me?

Am I attentive at Mass? Do I receive Communion with care and attention?

Have I worked unnecessarily on Sunday?

Have I missed attending Mass on Sundays or holy days of obligation?

Have I spoken God's name in disrespectful ways?

Have I respected and obeyed my elders, parents, employers, or teachers?

Have I physically harmed other people through acts of violence or neglect?

Have I committed any acts of violence?

Have I committed adultery?

Have I respected God's laws and the Church's laws concerning marriage?

Outside of marriage, have I shown another person affection in ways appropriate only between a husband and wife?

In marriage, am I open to having any children God may send?

Have I used artificial birth control to prevent God's creation of new life?

Have I taken anything that I had no right to take?

Have I pilfered office supplies or items belonging to my employer?

Have I shared all that I should — of my belongings, my time, my friendship?

Have I treated other people's property carelessly?

Have I said things that I knew would hurt someone?

Have I gossiped?

Have I lied?

Have I emphasized the negative qualities of other people or their work?

Have I spoken badly of the Church?

Have I boasted about myself or my work?

Have I been dishonest — with my employer, my family, the tax officials, or anyone else?

Have I placed false information on forms or in reports at work or at school? Is there anyone I have made to feel unwelcome in my presence?

In my thoughts or glances, have I invaded anyone's privacy in a way that would make them hurt or uncomfortable if they knew?

Have I used well the time and talents God has given me?

Have I offered my co-workers, friends, and family a good example of Christian life? Do I speak to them about God, and offer to pray with them or for them?

Do I tell people how much I appreciate them?

Do I pray every day for the repose of friends and family members who have died?

Are there people I have refused to forgive?

Do I dress modestly?

Have I envied other people for the things they own or the friends they have?

Have I allowed the desire for a better home or car, clothing or vacation, appliances or other material goods to disturb my inner peace?

Have I used another person for my own pleasure, convenience, or advancement?

# THOUGHTS ON CHRISTIAN FRIENDSHIP

"I call you friends."
— Jesus (John 15:15)

"Love one another as I have loved you."
— Jesus (John 15:12)

"There is no greater love than this, to lay down one's life for one's friends."
— Jesus (John 15:13)

"Let us show a friend our heart, and he will open his to us. . . . A friend, if he is true, hides nothing."
— St. Ambrose of Milan

"Rebukes are often better than silent friendship."
— St. Ambrose of Milan

"There is no greater invitation to love than loving first."
— St. Augustine

"Among our most notorious adversaries are people destined to be our friends."
— St. Augustine

"Rightly has a friend been called 'the half of my soul.'"
— St. Augustine

"There is no true friendship unless you weld it between souls that cleave together through the charity shed in our hearts by the Holy Spirit."
— St. Augustine

"Here is how a friend differs from a flatterer: the flatterer speaks to give pleasure, but the friend refrains from nothing, even that which gives pain."
— St. Basil the Great

"True friendship should never conceal what it thinks."
— St. Jerome

"True friendship can harbor no suspicion; a friend must speak to his friend as freely as to his second self."
— St. Jerome

"A friend is another self."
— St. Thomas Aquinas

"Friendships begun in this world will be taken up again, never to be broken off."
— St. Francis de Sales